THE CATHOLIC VOTE

CATHOLICS PARTICIPATING IN PUBLIC LIFE

THE CATHOLIC VOTE

CATHOLICS PARTICIPATING IN PUBLIC LIFE

LARRY T. O'NEILL

JEFFERSON HOUSE PUBLISHING

ILLINOIS

PUBLISHED BY JEFFERSON HOUSE
P.O. 2426
Palatine, IL 60078
www.jeffersonhousepublishing.com

Copyright © 2009 by Larry T. O'Neill

All Rights Reserved

Published in the United States by
JEFFERSON HOUSE PUBLISHING
Illinois

Book Design by ONE ILLustration, LLC

Cataloging-in-Publication Data

O'Neill, Larry T.
The Catholic Vote : catholics participating in public life
By Larry T. O'Neill. – 1st ed.
1. Catholic Church – United States – Political Activity
2. Catholicism and Politics
3. Church and state – United States. I. Title.

ISBN 978-1-61658-681-2

PRINTED IN THE UNITED STATES OF AMERICA

ACKNOWLEDGEMENTS

To the Lord Almighty who inspires us all and from whom all goodness flows.

My deep gratitude to my son, Michael, who assisted with editing, graphic design and layout.

I would like to express my deep appreciation to Father Paul Kais for his many timely suggestions and observations.

My sincere thanks to Les and Kathleen Miller for all of their inspirational thoughts and ideas to help with the final version of the book.

Finally, I want to thank my wife, Marilyn, for her encouragement, understanding and support.

PREFACE

Back in the year 2006, I wrote a letter to a Chicago area daily newspaper which simply asked the question: why are the American people anointing a relatively unknown State Senator from Illinois as our new Messiah and hope for the future when we know little or nothing about him or what he stands for?

Normally, when we evaluate prospective candidates, we look at their experience, their character, their ability to lead, their ability to make tough decisions, etc. But in this case, Barack Obama was the least experienced candidate to become a major party's nominee in recent memory.

Two years later in 2008, I saw this same candidate whom many voted for because he was the candidate of change become the President of the United States.

While many quickly got behind his promises to improve the economy or to create new jobs, what worried me more was what he was saying about the larger issues of life, liberty, religion and the family.

Candidate Obama in 2007 had actually promised a group of his supporters that if elected he would sign a bill - the Freedom of Choice Act (FOCA) – against which Cardinal Frances George, President of the U.S. Conference of Catholic Bishops, has spoken out clearly for the Catholic Bishops when he said:

> FOCA would coerce all Americans into subsidizing and promoting abortion with their tax dollars….it would counteract any and all sincere efforts by government and others of good will to reduce the number of abortions in our country…FOCA would have an equally destructive effect on the freedom of conscience of doctors, nurses and health care workers whose personal convictions do not permit them to cooperate in the private killing of unborn children. It would be an evil law that further divides our country, and the Church should be intent on opposing evil.

The Cardinal went on to say "abortion kills not only unborn children; it destroys constitutional order and the common good, which is assured only when the life of every human being is legally protected. Aggressively pro-abortion policies, legislation and executive orders will permanently alienate tens of millions of Americans, and would be seen by many as an attack on the free exercise of their religion".

This got my attention and was in part my inspiration to start writing this book about Catholics participating in public life.

As fate would have it, in late 2008 a Catholic group asked me if I would speak to them about this bill which was picking up steam in Washington and was the payback President Obama was giving to his supporters who very much wanted to permanently enshrine abortion into our law and our culture.

Immediately after my talk, a number of people in the audience approached me and asked me if I would consider putting my speech in print so that many others could be informed about the impending FOCA legislation and how devastating it would be to our whole nation and its people.

At that point I re-arranged my schedule so that I could spend five days a week researching, studying and writing about how detrimental this new legislation could be to America and try and awaken America to this impending danger.

Being Catholic myself, I realized how important a role the Catholic Church – both leaders and members - could play in fighting this legislation. My research led me to realize that the numbers showed that people who call themselves Catholic (but weren't even following the church on basic things like attending mass on Sundays) were in essence electing candidates such as Barack Obama. I simply want to help them to realize that as Catholics we have a huge stake in building and protecting this great republic we call the United States of America.

When we see that laws violate the natural law or our Catholic teaching such as the wanton destruction of human life , as with abortion, we have a responsibility as Catholics and citizens concerned with the common good to try to correct the injustice.

The title and contents of this book, "The Catholic Vote" does not in any way imply that there should be a monolithic Catholic vote on all issues. Natural law and a correct understanding of the common good should inform the voting decisions of all voters (including voters who are Catholic). The vast majority of other social and political issues are outside the realm of these principles and are subject to no official Church teaching. Catholics are free to vote their conscience on these other issues.

Catholics need to take a more active and vigorous role in public debate in America. We are an integral part of our nation's life and future. What better way for Catholics to build the future of this great Republic than by living their Catholic faith truly and authentically? For what good is your faith if it doesn't affect how you live your life?

TABLE OF CONTENTS

1. What Did the 2008 Elections Teach Us? 1
2. Getting Involved in the Political Process 10
3. What is a Truly Catholic Conscience? 17
4. Judicial Activism 35
5. Media 46
6. Culture versus The Economy 57
7. Whom Has America Forgotten? 66
8. Changing Our Existing Culture of Death to a Culture of Life 80

CHAPTER 1.

WHAT DID THE 2008 ELECTIONS TEACH US?

After our recent 2008 general election, millions of Catholics were wondering how America could elect the most militantly pro-abortion candidate ever to win a major party's presidential nomination and then go on to win the Presidency, the highest elected office in the land.

The demographics from this election were very revealing and not very flattering to Catholics who take the words of our Declaration of Independence seriously:

"We hold these truths to be self evident that all men are created equal and that they are endowed by their creator with certain inalienable rights that among these are LIFE, liberty and the pursuit of happiness".

Until recent times there has been little doubt why the founders of our nation who were predominantly Christian listed LIFE first among our inalienable rights. They knew that there is no such thing as the authority of government separate from the authority of God.

Even though most of our founders believed in God, they knew by their reason and the natural law what was the proper course of action in fighting for their personal freedom and eventually founding our country. Natural law teaches that all creation has a "nature", an inherent order and purpose. The natural law can be called the unwritten law of human nature. By using their reason, men and women can know what conforms to their human nature and is therefore good.

Haven Bradford Gow, a contributing editor of the Catholic League for Religious and Civil rights, puts it this way:

> Proponents of a natural law philosophy maintain that there is an objective moral order that is higher than the laws of the state and social customs and traditions; this natural moral law (which essentially is the Golden Rule and the Ten Commandments) is ascertainable through man's rational capacity and is applicable to all people, and in all times and in all places; this philosophy is reflected in the thinking and writings of this nation's Founding Fathers who affirmed a belief in the law of nature and of nature's God. Those who believe in a natural rights philosophy

insist that man is qualitatively different from mere animal and the rest of physical nature because he possesses free will, rationality, a soul and is made in the image and likeness of God. Because of the kind of being man is, he possesses intrinsic moral worth and dignity and unalienable rights like the rights to life, liberty, property and the pursuit of happiness. As affirmed in the Declaration of Independence, it is the government's obligation to preserve, protect and promote our unalienable rights. (1)

Charles Rice, former law professor at Notre Dame, affirms the necessary existence of a natural law when he says:

> Natural law will seem mysterious if we forget that everything has a law built into its nature. The nature of a rock is such that it will sink if you throw it into a pond. An automobile will function if you feed it gasoline... The natural law is the story of how things work.... Morality is governed by a law built into the nature of man and knowable by reason. Man can know, through the use of reason, what is in accord with his nature and therefore good. Every law, however, has to have a lawgiver. Let us say upfront that the natural law makes no ultimate sense without God as its author....The natural law is a set of manufacturer's directions written into our nature so that we can discover through reason how we ought to act. It is nothing other than the light of understanding infused in us by God, whereby we understand what must be done and what must be avoided. (2)

Through this "light of understanding" we can place our votes and support causes according to what we know in our hearts to be good (even without the aid of our religious beliefs). The natural and moral law doesn't change with the times - it only has different applications. Just as slavery was the defining issue of its time, abortion, which has taken the lives of almost 50 million unborn babies since the infamous Roe vs Wade decision of 1973, is the salient issue of our age.

John Paul II ended his pastoral visit to the United States in 1987 proclaiming:

> The best tradition of your land presumes respect for those who cannot defend themselves. If you want equal justice for all, and true freedom and lasting peace, then, America, defend life! All the great causes that are yours today will have meaning only to the extent that you guarantee the right to life and protect the human person..... Every human person—no matter how vulnerable or helpless, no matter how young or old, no matter how healthy, handicapped, or sick, no matter how useful or productive for society—is a being of inestimable worth created in the image and likeness of God. This is the dignity of America, the reason she exists, the condition for her survival—yes, the ultimate test of her greatness: to respect every human person, especially the weakest and most defenseless ones, those as yet unborn. (3)

John Paul II's words and witness to the intrinsic dignity of all human life have greatly impacted America especially considering the significant representation of Catholics amongst the populace of the United States. Roman Catholicism has grown in this country from a tiny minority of

1% of the population in the original thirteen colonies to approximately 24% in 2008. This is roughly four times larger than the Southern Baptist Convention, the next largest Christian denomination. (4) In 2008 there were 67.5 million registered members of the Roman Catholic Church. (5)

In 2008, 54% of Catholic voters who identify themselves as Catholic, one of the largest voting blocs in our nation, voted for the pro-abortion candidate. The even more meaningful statistic is that Catholic voters who attend mass weekly voted for the pro-life candidate by a less than impressive majority of only 54% to 45%. Finally, among those who do not attend weekly Mass, the pro-abortion candidate won by an overwhelming majority of 61% to 37%. (6) Clearly the pro-abortion candidate garnered his support from Catholics who were not following even the most basic practice of participating in the liturgy of their Church.

And therein lies the rub. People call themselves Catholic but are not even doing the minimum (i.e. attending Mass on Sunday) and are certainly not following the teachings of their Church on the most basic moral issues. One could make a great case that they are, in effect, electing the President of the United States.

It must be understood that there is no implication that the Catholic vote should be a monolithic vote on all issues.

Natural and moral law and a correct understanding of the common good should inform the voting decisions of all voters (including voters who are Catholic). The Catholic Church's position on some issues such as abortion, the direct taking of innocent life, are non-negotiable for Catholics and are upheld by natural and moral law principals. As the vast majority of other political and social issues are outside the realm of these principals and are subject to no official Church teaching. Catholics are free to vote their conscience on these issues.

The results of the voting patterns in the 2008 general election of people who call themselves Catholic should send shockwaves first of all to the United States Catholic Bishops who did publish a document entitled *Faithful Citizenship* which was intended to clarify the Church's position on abortion to the American electorate. Unfortunately, it failed to hit its mark for a number of reasons and potentially added to the confusion. Several bishops, including Archbishop Charles J. Chaput of Denver, have spoken out clearly and courageously on the moral obligations of all Catholics. Many Catholic voters ignored or were not aware of the Bishops' guidance. Putting their concerns of the economy ahead of their moral obligations, they elected a pro-abortion candidate.

In 2003 Cardinal Francis George of Chicago addressed the U.S. Bishops in St. Louis and said, "I would argue that the post-Vatican II Church's greatest failure is the failure to have formed and to call forth a laity engaged in the world in order to change it." He added, that the goal is "to form people with a genuine love of the city and love of the culture, itself." (6)

I believe that Cardinal George's evaluation is correct but it more importantly raises the issue that both the Bishops and the laity should take this opportunity to look in the mirror and not engage in the blame game. Each individual person should make a commitment to become more directly engaged in changing this existing culture of death to a culture of life.

If we are to change our current culture, it must be done primarily by lay people who live and work out in the world and therefore have the best opportunity to affect it. The continual worry of the laity about what has or has not been done in the past is self-defeating. We all have made our own mistakes or lacked the courage to speak out at certain times. The point is that our culture is teetering on the edge of collapse whether everyone realizes it or not. In America today approximately 1 million unborn babies are killed yearly in their mother's womb, 50% of marriages end in divorce, and four out of every 10 children are born out of wedlock. God gave each individual person the gifts of intellect and will - each of us can choose to make a difference.

Somehow we need to recapture the courage and will of our country's early founders who battled famine and hardship far greater than most Americans have ever seen. We must realize that our very lives and the lives of our families are at stake in this battle for the very soul of the United States of America. All of us (bishops, priests, religious & LAY PEOPLE) have to take the words of former President Theodore Roosevelt seriously and get engaged in this culture as if our very lives depended on it:

> It is not the critic who counts; not the man who points out how the strong man stumbles or where the doer of deeds could have done better. The credit belongs to the man who is actually in the arena, whose face is marred by dust and sweat and blood, who strives valiantly, who errs and comes up short again and again, because there is no effort without error of shortcoming, but who knows the great enthusiasms, the great devotions, who spends himself for a worthy cause; who, at the best, knows in the end, the triumph of high achievement, and who, at the worst, if he fails, at least he fails while daring greatly, so that his place shall never be with those cold and timid souls who knew neither victory nor defeat. (8)

Archbishop Chaput on February 8, 2009 addressed this very subject in Ireland in a speech entitled *Building and Promoting a Culture of Life: An American View*. He said:

Be ready to pay the ultimate price. Pope John Paul II very shrewdly choose St. Thomas More, a martyr, as the patron saint of lawyers and politicians. Thomas More and his friend Bishop John Fisher, both of them executed by the same king for their fidelity to the Catholic faith, are models of how far we should be willing to go for our beliefs. In today's world, we may never be asked to pay the ultimate price. But we do see character assassination and calumny against good people every day in the public media. And we should be ready to pay that price too. (9)

CHAPTER 2.

GETTING INVOLVED IN THE POLITICAL PROCESS

When Paul Revere rode through the streets of Boston warning the early colonists that "the British are coming, the British are coming", he was giving his fellow Americans a wake up call to stand up and defend our nation. This book is an attempt to act as a catalyst for all those who love America to take a stand for life, liberty and the pursuit of happiness for ourselves, our families and all future generations who love freedom so much they are willing to fight and even die for it. As Americans, eventually we all have to ask ourselves (as did the early colonists when the British were imposing their will on the people) when do we make a stand for the things that are most important to us and our families?

I made that decision back in the 1970's and here is one example of how I, as a Catholic layman, tried to get involved in the Public Square.

The year was 1975 and I was working for 3M Company based in St. Paul, MN. Part of my duties required frequent travel. One night I was staying at a hotel up in Milwaukee, WI and I was watching a late night talk show program being hosted by David Frost. One of the guests was a Dr. Mildred Jefferson, a black woman with Harvard Law and Medical Degrees. She was debating 3 people who favored abortion rights. Dr. Jefferson literally verbally destroyed their specious pro-abortion arguments until finally one of the panelists conceded defeat and basically said they could not compete with her. I was so shocked that I picked up the phone and called my wife. As it turns out she had been watching the very same program. We both wondered how this barbaric procedure could be happening in America without public outcry?

The answer at the time was not clear to me but it is today. The major media is the most powerful force in our secular culture today. Dr. Mildred Jefferson was never to appear again on a similar nationally televised secular debate format again. The simple truth of the matter is that she was too good and the major secular media has an agenda to protect. Believe me, they are not pro-life.

How do I know this? I have many examples of media bias that it would take up the rest of this book so I will just share one story with you that Joe Sheidler, a national pro-life activist, shared with me. Back in the 1980's Joe attended a conference out in Aspen, Colorado of the major media moguls—the big guns of Hollywood and the secular media. What Joe learned was astonishing because they openly admitted their plan of attack. They openly favored a push for unlimited abortion rights, admitting that sexual activity was synonymous with Hollywood. They needed abortion as a back up system - the major secular media would run interference for them.

When I got back from my business trip from Milwaukee, I immediately got involved in the pro-life movement. In 1977 I was still working and traveling for 3M Company but I also started working with Ralph Rivera as a pro-life lobbyist in Springfield, IL.

In 1976, Henry Hyde, a former Illinois Congressman, passed a bill in Congress called the Hyde Amendment that cut off all federal funds for abortion for people who could not afford the procedure. Individual states, such as Illinois, were trying to pass state laws limiting state funding of abortions. On the night before the expected vote in the Illinois Senate in Springfield, I was back in Chicago and Ralph was down in Springfield. At about 3:00 am, the morning of the expected vote, I jumped out of bed and declared to my wife that I was going down to Springfield for the vote. I could tell that she thought I was having a dream.

I finally got down to Springfield about 12:30 pm and Ralph Rivera informed me the vote had already been taken. We had lost. He told me that my state senator, Jack Graham, had switched his vote at the last minute and caused the defeat of our bill. I went straight to Graham's office and his secretary informed me that the Senator was not seeing anyone today and that he was not feeling well. I walked right past her desk and opened the senator's door and said, "Jack, why in world did you vote against our pro-life bill?". He said that his office had gotten a flood of letters, phone-calls and telegrams saying that the people in his district were in favor of state funding for abortions.

At this point, his secretary was trying to get me out of his office saying he couldn't talk anymore. I immediately found a telephone outside of his office and called Bernie Pedersen, the local committeeman in my area, and asked him to immediately call Senator Graham and to get many others in the district to call also. I also called my wife who got the phones humming down to Springfield.

Within 30 minutes Jack Graham's secretary found me and said, "Jack says he gives up, call off all the phone calls - he will switch his vote in the Senate."

Fortunately, one of our pro-life senators put the bill on a recall agenda. Later that day the bill came up for another vote. This time Senator Graham voted to end all state funding of abortions in Illinois and he got up on the Senate floor and spoke in favor of the bill. The bill passed this time.

One of the sweetest moments for us was right after the bill passed when Ralph and I looked across the Senate floor at all the pro-abortion attorneys and lobbyists. They were stunned in disbelief that the bill passed this time. There was no time for a recall vote so the bill passed the full Senate. Eventually, this Illinois Senate Bill and the Hyde Amendment were ruled constitutional in 1980 by the United States Supreme Court. By cutting off all state funding of abortions we were able to save literally hundreds and perhaps thousands of unborn babies.

Back in the late 1970's, Thomas Roeser, former Vice President of Quaker Oats and President of the City Club of Chicago, called me and invited me to attend a City Club

Meeting featuring Senator Edward Kennedy of Massachusetts at the M & M Club in the Chicago Merchandise Mart.

Since the Kennedy family owned the Merchandise Mart, the audience was made up mainly of labor people and Democrats who were all loyal to their party and to the Massachusetts Senator. He looked very comfortable and relaxed in front of such a friendly crowd.

I was driving into the city and arrived late for the luncheon. When I walked into the M & M Club hall, I realized that all the seats were already taken except for one seat that was at a table with local black teachers and educators. I quickly introduced myself and sat down for the luncheon exchanging pleasantries about the weather, the Chicago sports scene and the current state of education in Chicago. Finally the meal was over and Roeser stepped to the microphone to select who would ask the Senator some questions. Senator Kennedy jumped to his feet (probably realizing that Roeser was a Republican) and told him that he would choose the questioners. The Senator looked to his left and as a sea of hands went up he selected someone who asked the first question. He then looked over to the right side of the audience where I was seated and another 75 hands went up. Senator Kennedy looked right at me and asked "what is your question?"

I said, "Senator Kennedy I understand that you have voted to support Medicare funding for abortion in the U.S. Senate". At that moment Senator Kennedy's expression changed into a serious frown and all the background buzzing in the audience fell deathly silent. I continued by saying that some of the major black leaders in the Chicago area like Jesse Jackson and Reverend Riddick said that Medicaid funding of abortion was akin to "extermination of the black race." (Jesse Jackson back in the 1970's was espousing a pro-life position on abortion. He has subsequently changed his position.) Needless to say at that point you could hear a pin drop in the audience. Senator Kennedy made a very feeble attempt to answer the question but never came close to a reasonable response that made sense to anyone in the audience. I'm sure the question was a total shock to the young senator who probably felt that this friendly audience would never ask such a direct question. After a lengthy pause, Senator Kennedy demanded a new question, basically ignoring mine and trying to change the subject as quickly as he could. The next time I ran into Tom Roeser, he mentioned that as Senator Kennedy was leaving the stage with him that day, the senator looked at him and said "that was quite a question on abortion."

CHAPTER 3.

WHAT IS A TRULY CATHOLIC CONSCIENCE?

Unfortunately millions of Catholics either do not fully understand what it is to have a well-formed Catholic conscience, that is, judgment guided by right reason and formed in the true teachings of the Church. Or they confuse the relationship between personal freedom and moral truth. Any credible theologian would agree that conscience is the lynch pin between man and his Creator. The Catholic faith has never taught that respect for conscience gives individuals absolute certitude in arriving at their own truth, or that anyone's beliefs are as good as others. Our conscience is not an independent or separate authority to do whatever we want to do or we feel like doing.

Catholic teaching specifically rejects the doctrine of "primacy of conscience" when conscience contradicts the most basic moral teachings of the Church. The desire to follow one's conscience does not give a person the right to erroneously and subjectively interpret the teachings of Christ and His Church. As Catholics we must form our conscience in accordance with authentic Catholic teaching.

Cardinal George Pell, Archbishop of Sydney and the highest-ranking prelate in the Catholic Church in Australia said, "This simply means we cannot accept a settled position against the Church on a basic moral teaching. Any difficulty with church teaching should not be the end of the matter but the beginning of a process of conversion, education and quite possibly repentance." (1)

Our conscience can be either right or wrong. The *Catechism of the Catholic Church* teaches that it must be informed or enlightened. A person who has not studied or learned the basic moral teachings of the Catholic Church more than likely has an uninformed or perhaps dead conscience. We need to form our conscience to the objective norm of truth. If our conscience is formed accordingly we can truly say "the truth will set us free".

The Catholic Church always has and always will teach that abortion is the taking of innocent human life, marriage is between one man and one woman and embryonic stem cell research is intrinsically evil because it ends the life of a human being. The Church speaks out on these issues not because they are "Catholic" issues but because they are moral issues. Bishop Robert Morlino of Madison, Wisconsin says:

> (these church teachings) are universal truths based on reason alone. They are based on the fact that every human person has an unsurpassed dignity; upon the fact that every human being is sacred from the moment from conception to natural death....There are things in this world which, we can know by our reason alone. Some things are objectively true and some things are intrinsically good—based in the first place on reason. This search for, and recognition of, the truth can never be based on my subjective opinions, emotions or desires at the time. The truth stands outside of us, to be seen and recognized. When we recognize the objective truth, we need to reconcile ourselves to the truth, never the other way around—this is the natural law". (2)

Richard John Neuhaus analyzes John Paul II's *The Splendor of Truth* by explaining how adherence to the moral law gives real freedom. He explains the truth about freedom:

> Modernity, he notes appreciatively, has been very big on freedom. But now freedom has been untethered from truth, and freedom cannot stand alone without degenerating into license. License, in turn, is the undoing of freedom, for then, as Nietzsche and others recognized,

all personal and social life becomes simply the assertion of power. If freedom is to be secured, power—and freedom itself—must be accountable to truth. Or, as John Paul puts it repeatedly, "Authentic freedom is ordered to truth." (3)

The greatest example that I can think of for the Catholic layman is St. Thomas More, the patron saint of lawyers and politicians, who paid the ultimate price in his martyrdom for his beliefs. He formed his conscience according to the teachings of the Catholic Church and was able to witness to the truth in spite of false testimony given against him at his trial. We all must follow our consciences in our own particular cases as this saint did but conscience itself is judged and inspired by the moral law. Thomas More and Henry VIII both followed their consciences. Thomas More became a Saint; Henry VIII we leave to God's mercy.

Throughout American history, great moral issues such as slavery have faced our nation. Our Declaration of Independence reminds us of the importance of equality and life: "we hold these truths to be self evident: that all men are created equal; that they are endowed by their Creator with certain unalienable rights; that among them are life." Today in the United States of America we also have great moral issues facing our nation that endanger the very lives of our citizens.

Catholic Moral Teaching is crystal clear in defending four of the great moral issues of our day:

1) MARRIAGE - MARRIAGE IS BETWEEN ON MAN AND ONE WOMAN. PERIOD
2) EMBRYONIC STEM CELL RESEARCH - A human embryo is a human being (even if produced by cloning). We simply cannot kill another human being.
3) IN VITRO FERTILIZATION - God wants life to be the result of the act of love in marriage by those committed to loving each other. Every human embryo that is used in multiple implantations that is discarded or destroyed is the loss of another human life.
4) ABORTION - WE CANNOT KILL INNOCENT, DEFENSELESS BABIES.

MARRIAGE

The Catechism of the Catholic Church defines marriage as "the matrimonial covenant, by which a man and a woman establish between themselves a partnership of the whole of life, is by its nature ordered toward the good of the spouses and the procreation and education of offspring; this covenant between baptized persons has been raised by Christ the Lord to the dignity of a sacrament." (4)

Saint Josemaria Escrivá de Balaguer in *Marriage: A Christian Institution* writes:

> For a Christian marriage is not just a social institution, much less a mere remedy for human weakness. It is a real supernatural calling. A great sacrament, in Christ and in the Church, says St. Paul (cf Eph 5:3). At the same time, it is a permanent contract between a man and woman. Whether we like it or not, the sacrament of matrimony, instituted by Christ, cannot be dissolved. It is a permanent contract that sanctifies in cooperation with Jesus Christ. He fills the souls of husband and wife and invites them to follow him. He transforms their married life into an occasion for God's presence on earth. Husband and wife are called to sanctify their married life and to sanctify themselves in it. (5)

Even though marriage is recognized by the vast majority of Americans as a life long union of one man and one woman who enter into a total sharing of themselves for the sake of family a well funded, vocal minority in America with the tacit support of the secular media are trying to make us believe that gay marriage and civil unions are in the "common good" of society.

WHAT IS A TRULY CATHOLIC CONSCIENCE? / 23

A 2004 statement by five Dutch Social Science professors on the deterioration of Marriage in the Netherlands seems to refute the good news that our secular media beams to us almost on a daily basis:

> Until the late 1980's marriage was a flourishing institution in the Netherlands. The number of marriages was high, the number of divorces was relatively low compared to other Western countries, and the number of illegitimate births also was low. It seems, however; that legal and social experiments in the 1990's have had an adverse effect on the reputation of man's most important institution.
>
> Over the past fifteen years, the number of marriages has declined substantially, both in absolute and in relative terms. In 1990, 95,000 marriages were solemnized (6.4 marriages per 1,000 inhabitants); by 2003, that number had dropped to 82,000 (5.1 marriages per 1,000 inhabitants).
>
> The same period also witnessed a spectacular rise in the number of illegitimate births. In 1989 one in ten children were born out of wedlock (11%); by 2003, that number had risen to almost one in three (31%). The number of never-married people grew by more than 850,000, from 6.46 million in 1990 to 7.32 million in 2003.

The Dutch professors continue:

> People seem to attach less importance to marriage. More people are having children out of wedlock, even though marriage is the best setting for successfully raising a child. There is a broad base of social and legal research that shows marriage to be the best structure for the successful raising of children. A child of out-of-wedlock parents has a greater chance of experiencing problems in his or her

psychological development, health, school performance, and even the quality of future relationships... there are good reasons to believe that the decline in Dutch marriage may be connected to the successful public campaign for the opening of marriage to same-sex couples in the Netherlands... We call upon politicians, academics, and opinion leaders to acknowledge the facts that marriage in the Netherlands is now an endangered institution and that the many children born out of wedlock are likely to suffer the consequences of that development. (6)

The Netherlands experimented with social change back in the nineties and we see the devastating results ten years later. All the historical evidence (legal and social) points out that marriage between one man and one woman is far and away the best setting to raise children and yet where have we ever heard that mentioned in our secular society today? Was this study ever given the light of day in the American media? Of course not - the secular media basically favors same sex marriage. The consequence to our families is extremely detrimental.

As of 2009, four states (Massachusetts, Connecticut, Vermont, and Iowa) have now legalized gay marriage. When State Supreme Courts or extremely liberal legislatures like in the case of Vermont fail to follow the natural moral law, we will continue to get same sex marriage. However, once the people get involved, such as in state constitutional amendments where all the people can participate, then we have a totally different story. Thomas Jefferson once said, "Whenever the people are well informed, they can be trusted with their own government; whenever things get so far wrong as to attract their notice, they may be relied upon to set them to right". (7)

In the 31 states where the American people have actually voted for a state constitutional amendment that simply says marriage is between one man and one women, American citizens by a resounding total of 31 states to 0 have rejected gay marriage. They understand the issue by their faith and their reason that gay marriage is not in the best interests of children and families. Most importantly it goes against God's natural law. Let us be clear that the American people have not okayed gay marriage even though the media and a well financed minority would lead us to believe that America supports gay marriage. Marriage between one man and one woman has been the core building block of every society for thousands of years.

STEM CELL RESEARCH

One moral issue that has confused millions of Catholics and Americans is stem cell research. Dr. Amin Abboud, an Australian bioethicist at the University of New South Wales in Sydney and the director of Australasian Bioethics Information, clarifies the issue by saying:

> Regenerative medicine is an exciting new field of medicine where different techniques are used in trying to repair damaged organs and tissues. Stem cell therapy is one avenue of regenerative medicine...The ethical issue is not whether stem cells can bring about cures but rather where the stem cells come from." The aspect of the debate that most people don't realize is that stem cells come in two varieties—adult stem cells (whose exploration pose no moral dilemma) and embryonic stem cells (those whose study require the destruction of a human embryo). Once again we see an issue driven by the media which is heavily slanted toward the funding of basically all types of embryonic stem cell research. Only tacit coverage has been given to the benefits of adult stem cell research and the great moral dilemma over the destruction of a human embryo has typically been glossed over.

Dr. Abboud continues that:

> The destruction of embryos for stem cells for stem cell research is ethically unacceptable....Researching on embryos is researching on embryonic persons. It denies the dignity of the human embryo. The human embryo is a distinct, living human being, and is entitled to all the rights and protections as any other human being. Human life begins at conception (or fertilization). Therefore, the human embryo (regardless of what means by which it was created) should not be treated as a means to an end. It is entitled to life and respect. Once embryonic development commences, a separate and distinct being exists which should not be used in a purely instrumental fashion. For this reason any technology or proposed therapeutic procedure which involves the destruction of a human embryo should be banned altogether. (8)

I believe that we need to do a better job of recognizing that a human embryo is a human being (even if produced by cloning). Once this is accepted, it is easy to see that it is simply wrong to use human beings in hopes of curing others. The major difficulty at the core of the embryonic stem-cell research is that a five-day old human being must be destroyed to obtain embryonic stem cells. All civilizations have known by the natural moral law that the idea of destroying a young member of the human family is always wrong and immoral. The Catholic Church has been one of the lone voices attempting to get both the ethical and human issues out in front of the public for a complete hearing.

The issue has been hijacked by political parties for their own gain. As an example, shortly after paralyzed actor Christopher Reeve of Superman fame died, a prominent candidate argued that, "if we do the work that we can do in this country - assuming the right political party is elected - people like Christopher Reeve are going to walk, get up out of that wheelchair and walk again." (9) Of course that was lofty language and not medically possible. Charles Krauthammer, a medical doctor and also a victim of paralysis, says "rhetoric like this is nothing more than pandering to the hopes of suffering and desperate people for political gain, without any real prospect of delivering on those hopes. Claims of impending miracle cures based on embryonic stem cell research are simply false. In fact, no such hope exists anywhere in the foreseeable future." (10)

We do know that the biotech industry was unable to gain significant private funding for its research because venture capitalists saw little or no hope of success with embryonic stem cells. Bio-ethicists instead decided to seek major funding from state taxpayers such as in the case of California's Proposition 71. They spent nearly $25 million to persuade the electorate to borrow $3 billion over 10 years to fund therapeutic cloning research and experiments with embryonic stem cells. (11) The ironic part of this is that California has a massive billion dollar deficit and hospitals and emergency rooms are closing because they have no money. Somehow they can pass a 3 billion dollar boondoggle that is totally unnecessary considering the scientific developments involving adult stem cells, umbilical cord blood stem cells, or tissue from other sources have produced tremendous cures. We hear of new medical breakthroughs using adult stem cells on a regular basis.

Embryonic stem cell research is plain and simple bogus science. The Catholic Church has no problem with true science. It believes in methodical and true science in all branches of knowledge, provided it is carried out in a truly scientific manner and does not override moral laws, such as the killing of another human being.

The bottom line is that, in fact, NO cures have resulted from this extravagant waste of money with embryonic stem cell research. The next time you become involved in a discussion on embryonic stem cell research simply ask the person who thinks that is such a good idea: (1) why does the human immune system reject these newly undeveloped cells? (2) why do the embryonic stem cells from so many tumors when transplanted to adult tissue? and (3) why has science provided essentially no convincing evidence that embryonic stem cells can be reliably differentiated into normal adult cell types?

One of the key points in this whole debate that all Catholics and Christians need to emphasize is that three of the four stem cell types pose NO moral dilemma and ADULT stem cells have cured thousands of actual people with (heart disease, cancer, Parkinson's disease, stroke, leukemia, lupus, rheumatoid arthritis, etc). New scientific medical evidence now documents that adult stem cells and umbilical cord stem cells can treat men and woman with serious illnesses without compromising any moral barriers.

Charles Krauthammer, medical doctor, journalist, and member of the President's Council on Bioethics in an article entitled, "Stem Cell Vindication" said that:

> "A decade ago (James A.) Thomson was the first to isolate human embryonic stem cells. Last week, he (and Japan's Shinya Yamanaka) announced one of the great breakthroughs since the discovery of DNA: an embryonic freeway to produce genetically matched stem cells. Even a scientist who cares not a whit about the morality of embryo destruction will adopt this technique because it is simple and powerful. The embryonic stem cell debate is over….That holy grail has now been achieved. Largely because of the genius of Thomson and Yamanaka. And also because of the astonishing good fortune that nature requires only four injected genes to turn an ordinary adult skin cell into a magical stem cell that can become bone or brain or heart or liver." (12)

One of the great mysteries of this century is why so many politicians, media and other influential people constantly push embryonic stem cell research when adult stem cells can do the same thing without all the medical dangers to the implanted person or the grave moral issues. There is no longer any debate as science has discovered a simple cost effective way to convert ordinary skin cells into pluripotent stem cells with the multi-faceted ability to develop into almost any kind of cell in the human body. The answer may lie in the November 2006 cloning initiative where billionaire

James Stowers Jr. contributed $9.5 million, including 4 million that was spent to collect signatures (13) to get the *Missouri Stem Cell Research and Cures Initiative* on the ballot.

The anti-life movement outspends the pro-lifers by millions of dollars every year. That is just another reason why every person who is against the killing of the youngest members of our human family needs to first of all get better educated on this vital issue. All pro-life people need to counter the millions of dollars that are being spent to destroy human life with the truth that embryonic stem cell research is a total fraud and is no longer even a viable alternative in light of these scientific advances. Everyone who believes in the sanctity of human life doesn't need to wait for someone else to "step up to the plate" or use the common cop out that "my pastor never talks about the abortion issue". That's not the point! Each human person is endowed by our Creator with certain unalienable rights and we all need to take responsibility for this human holocaust that now is approaching 50 million unborn babies just by abortion in America.

Catholic Archbishop Raymond L. Burke had this to say on August 28, 2006. The initiative is "an attack on the natural moral law which God has written upon our hearts. He teaches us to safeguard and defend and foster human life from the moment of its inception to the moment of natural death. The initiative denies the fundamental right to life to a whole class of human beings on the basis of their size and inability to defend themselves." (14)

IVF

Unfortunately another issue where Catholics and the American people are not very well informed is In Vitro Fertilization (IVF). It is a medical technique that enables infertile couples to have children and has become widely accepted in the general public. The grave moral problems that exist have been widely ignored or downplayed by the media. The case of Nadya Suleman who gave birth to eight babies (octuplets) on January 26, 2009 has focused the spotlight on this very troubling but basically misunderstood issue. Many Catholics, unaware of the immense moral problems that emanate from IVF, must recognize the practice as a violation of God's plan for procreation and an offense against human dignity. In nearly every in vitro fertilization procedure there are unused embryos. John Haas, the editor of The National Catholic Bioethics Center, explains that "It is estimated that there are approximately 500,000 cryopreserved (frozen) embryos in the United States for possible use in the future...Children are gifts from a loving Father and not something to which couples have a right. They come to families from God as "mysterious strangers" to use the characterization of Leon Kass; they are not another commodity that may be custom-designed to satisfy our consumer preferences." (15) Only God truly knows what will become of these tiny human beings. Catholics must become better educated and more resolute in defending their moral opposition to IVF. The bottom line is that a human embryo is a human being and we cannot kill another human being.

ABORTION:

John T. Noonan writes in his book, *A Private Choice*, "Once or twice in a century an issue arises so divisive in its nature, so far-reaching in its consequences and so deep in its foundations that it calls every person to take a stand. This issue has not gone away as many predicted it would. Today it divides the country... Legalized as a private act, abortion has become a public issue. It has become the kind of public issue that compels almost everyone to take a stand." (16)

Abortion takes the life of a living, breathing human being. Since the infamous *Roe v Wade* decision in 1973, the total number of deaths of unborn babies is nearing 50 million.

Mother Theresa once said "abortion is a crime that kills not only the child but the consciences of all involved". (17)

In a letter to the US Supreme Court on Roe v. Wade, she said:

> As your Declaration of Independence put it, in words that have never lost their power to stir the heart... A nation founded on these principles holds a sacred trust: to stand as an example to the rest of the world, to climb ever higher in its practical realization of the ideals of human dignity, brotherhood, and mutual respect. Your constant efforts in fulfillment of that mission, far more than your size or your wealth or your military might, have made America an inspiration to all mankind....Yet there has been one infinitely tragic and destructive departure from these American ideals in recent memory. It was the Court's own decision in Roe v. Wade (1973) to exclude the unborn child from the human family. You ruled that a mother, in consultation with her doctor, has broad discretion, guaranteed against infringement by the United States Constitution, to choose to destroy her unborn child...Human rights are not a privilege conferred by government. They are every human being's entitlement by virtue of his humanity. The right to life does not depend, and must not be declared to be contingent, on the pleasure of anyone else, not even a parent or a sovereign. (18)

CHAPTER 4.

JUDICIAL ACTIVISM

The basic question we, as freedom loving Americans, have to ask ourselves in this current day is: can we long endure if our imperial, unelected judiciary, continues to make laws, such as an unlimited right to abortion, gay marriage and the removal of God's name and presence from the public square?

America is increasingly being ruled not by law or by our duly elected representatives but by unaccountable judges who are destroying the very fabric of what once made America great. Think about it. When you go into the voting booth next time and pull the lever for a judge, do you know anything about what that person stands for except his name and his political party? The fact of the matter is that our early founders were cognizant of the potential danger of a runaway judiciary when Alexander Hamilton wrote in the *Federalist Papers* "that he expected Congress to use its 'discretion' to make appropriate 'exceptions and regulations' to keep the judiciary 'the least dangerous' of the three branches of government." (1)

At the beginning of the 19th century, the courts tried to assert their dominance over the legislative and executive branches of government. In 1802, with the assistance of the outgoing Federalist Party, they tried to stack the judiciary by doubling the number of federal circuit court judges from 17 to 35. Thomas Jefferson and the Jeffersonians quickly responded to this post-election court packing by passing the Judiciary Act which eliminated all 18 new federal circuit court judgeships.

The question that must be asked today is: why is our current Congress (U.S. House of Representatives and the U.S. Senate) so reluctant to challenge the power of the imperial judiciary when there is ample law and precedence on their side?

Newt Gingrich, former Speaker of the House of Representatives, in his book *Winning the Future* says "Over the last 50 years the Supreme Court has become a permanent constitutional convention in which the whims of five appointed lawyers have rewritten the meaning of the Constitution. Under this new all-powerful model of the Court, the Constitution and the law can be redefined with no boundaries." (2)

As many people realize but may have forgotten, amending the Constitution is a herculean task in our modern day of partisan politics. In order to pass an amendment, there needs to be a 2/3rd vote in both houses of congress and ratification by the legislature of ☐'s of the states. Gingrich addresses this:

> Yet all this effort is matched by a 5 to 4 vote on the Supreme Court. If five justices decide we cannot say "one nation under God", cannot pray at graduation, and cannot criticize politicians with campaign ads just before an election, then we lose these rights. If they decide that child pornography on the internet is protected by free speech (unlike prayer and political speech) that becomes the law of the land. This power grab by the court is a modern phenomenon and a dramatic break from all previous American history". (3)

Unfortunately in our current political environment we have become a country controlled by judicial activists who create their own law out of thin air and then cram it down our throats. Our founding fathers never intended for the courts to make law. The Constitution created the separation of powers of the federal government through the division into three branches: legislative, executive and judicial. The early founders of this country in their wisdom vested all legislative powers in the Congress. No legislative powers were granted to the courts. Yet in the past 50 years, the courts have become the predominant social policy making body in this nation. The recent history of the courts has provided us with some of the most deeply offensive laws to society, the morals of our country, and especially to Christians.

Here is just a short list of laws that our imperial judiciary has imposed on us:

- Wide Spread Pornography
- Removal of the Ten Commandments from public parks and buildings
- Suppression of the pledge of allegiance in public schools
- Unlimited right to abortion
- Gay marriage

The rulings of the courts have been out of touch with the views of the American people. For example, a Harris Poll conducted in December 2008 on abortion reveals where the American people actually stand on this grave moral issue:

- 95% of Americans say they favor laws ensuring only licensed physicians should do abortions.
- 88% favor informed consent laws that provide women with information about abortion risks and alternatives beforehand.
- 76% want laws that protect doctors and nurses from being forced to perform or refer for abortion against their will.
- 73% of Americans support parental involvement laws.
- 68% favor a ban on partial birth abortion.
- 63% favor bans on taxpayer-funded abortions. (4)

Professor Doug Kimec of Pepperdine University says "Recent cases dealing with homosexuality, dealing with same-sex marriage, dealing with very sensitive topics, suggest the judges are all too willing sometimes to impose their own views merely because others in other nations agree with them." (5) This idea agrees perfectly with what Justice Anthony Kennedy said in *Roper v Simmons*, a juvenile death penalty case, in March, 2005 "existing standards, values are no longer any good because of values we share with a wider civilization." (6) Supreme Court Justice Antonin Scalia has made the general observation that "unelected judges have no place deciding issues such as abortion and the death penalty. The Courts 5 to 4 ruling March 1st to outlaw the juvenile death penalty based on 'evolving notions of decency' was simply a mask for the personal preferences of the 5 member majority." (7)

Scalia's point is that issues like abortion and the juvenile death penalty are issues that should be decided at the ballot box and by our elected representatives not by 5 unelected lawyers who have lifetime appointments. Justice Robert Bork seems to concur: "The struggle over the Supreme Court is not just about law; it is about the future of the culture". (8)

Since our culture involves our values, our faith and our total everyday existence, it is impossible to discuss activist judges without looking at how they affect our religious freedom and our very lives.

Archbishop Charles J. Chaput while accepting a recent Canterbury award addressed the issue of losing our religious freedom. He had this to say:

> More than any other country in the world, the United States is a nation that only makes sense in a religion-friendly context. The writer Robert D. Kaplan... once said that America has done so well for so long because her

founders had a tragic sense of history. They had few illusions about human perfectibility. And they got that spirit from the world of faith that shaped their experience.

The Archbishop continues:

The founders certainly had hope in their ability to build a "new order of things"—but only under the judgment of a creator. In other words, they had a sane kind of hope; the biblical kind that's grounded in realism, because they all believed in sin. They had an unsentimental grasp of weakness and flaws that need to be constrained. And that kind of thinking had very practical, political results. American ideals require a certain kind of citizen to make them work. That's why John Adams said that "Our constitution was made only for a moral and religious people. It is wholly inadequate to the government of any other. (9)

One issue that has caused considerable confusion not only among the electorate but also among legal scholars is the courts' interpretation of the term "separation of church and state".

Richard John Neuhaus in 1984 authored a book entitled "The Naked Public Square" that shifted the debate for religious intellectuals in America. This work was described by

Fr. Raymond J. De Souza as "an argument against the idea that American constitutional law required the banishment of religion from public life. The separation of church and state, Father Neuhaus argued over several decades, was precisely to allow maximum freedom for the free exercise of religion, and in a democratic, pluralist society, that meant plenty of room for religious voice in public life." (10)

Timothy George, a writer for the Evangelical magazine *Christianity Today*, espouses a similar view of Neuhaus's convictions:

> Neuhaus argued that the constitutional separation of church and state was meant to protect private practice but also enhance—not prohibit—the "free exercise" of religion in public life...Moreover, our most cherished political principals—including the irreducible value of persons, free speech, and religious liberty, resistance to tyranny, and respect for the rule of law—are all grounded in religiously informed beliefs. (11)

Our first amendment clearly states that "Congress shall make no law respecting an establishment of religion or prohibiting the free exercise thereof." Our founders simply wanted to prevent Congress from establishing an official national religion. That is why they established "freedom to worship" as one of our first and most basic rights. Thomas Jefferson and James Madison are usually considered the least religious of the early Presidents, yet both attended church services in the Capitol. As a matter of fact almost all the signers of the Declaration of Independence believed in God and they worshipped in their own individual churches.

We have a great heritage in this country of people of faith getting involved in public life and ascending to the highest offices in the land. In recent years, the notion of the separation of church and state has been hijacked by some, taking it well beyond its original meaning. They seek to remove faith and any acknowledgement of God from the public domain. Religion is seen as merely a private affair with no place in public life. It appears these people are set on establishing a new religion in America called secular humanism.

Following is a very short list of Supreme Court Decisions which many believe the courts have misinterpreted by an activist mentality thus creating law out of thin air. The courts were not established to create law but to interpret it. Many other Supreme Court cases exist where the courts have taken an activist position but space prevents them from being listed.

1) *Engel v. Vitale*, 82 S. Ct. 1261 (1962). (Prayer of any kind compiled by Public School Districts, even nondenominational prayer, is unconstitutional.)

2) *Abington School District v. Schempp*, 374 U.S. 203 (1963). (The Supreme Court concluded that any bible reading over the school intercom was unconstitutional.)

3) *Stone v. Graham*, 449 U.S. 39 (1980). (The Supreme Court said that any public display of the Ten Commandments in schools was unconstitutional.)

4) *Allegheny County v. ACLU*, 492 U.S. 573 (1989). (The Supreme Court ruled that any nativity scene displayed inside a government building violates the Establishment Clause.) (12)

Henry Hyde, long-time U.S. Congressman, patriot and a departed friend, explains in his book *For Every Idle Silence* just how far the secularists will go to push the envelope regarding separation of church and state.

> One evening I attended mass at St. Thomas More Cathedral in Arlington, Virginia, not far from my home in Falls Church. Bishop Thomas Welsh of Arlington was presiding at a mass to pray for the preservation of the lives of the unborn and had invited me to attend. I did so gladly. Unknown to me and others at the mass, I was followed into church by a private investigator working for the plaintiffs in the Hyde Amendment suit. He took notes. He watched me get up to read the epistle at mass, take communion, and appear to pray. He even followed me to a reception in the church hall afterward where I chatted with other pro-life people.

Congressman Hyde continues: "The private eye went so far as to write down a famous quotation written on a statue of St. Thomas More, one of my heroes and patron of the cathedral: "I die the king's servant but God's first".

These observations went into an affidavit that the plaintiffs attempted to introduce in court as yet more evidence of a religious conspiracy. They argued that the Hyde Amendment was unconstitutional because its principal sponsor was a devout Catholic who could not separate his religious beliefs from his political activity.

Hyde concludes his comments by saying "some powerful members of the cultural elites in our country are so paralyzed by the fear that theistic notions might reassert themselves in the official activities of government that they will go to Gestapo lengths to inhibit such expression". (13) Henry Hyde was a brave American who in my opinion was a real hero. We need more God-fearing men and women to step up and get involved in public life and not be cowed by this false interpretation of this great wall of separation that exists between church and state.

CHAPTER 5.

Media

Alexander Solzhenitsyn, the great Russian author and patriot who spent eight years in the Russian "Gulag", delivered the commencement address at Harvard University on June 8, 1978. The title of his talk was "A World Split Apart".

Solzhenitsyn, as an accomplished writer and visitor to America, brings a keen insight into American's elite media that is rarely encountered in our country's journalistic circles. In commenting on the direction of the American press, he says,

> The press...enjoys the widest freedom. There is no moral responsibility for deformation or disproportion. What sort of responsibility does a journalist have to his readers, or to history? If they have misled public opinion or the

government by inaccurate information or wrong conclusions, do we know of any cases of public recognition and rectification of such mistakes by the same journalists or the same newspapers? No, it does not happen, because it would damage sales. A nation may be the victim of such a mistake, but the journalist always gets away with it. One may safely assume that he will start writing the opposite with renewed self-assurance.

Solzhenitsyn continues:

Because instant and credible information has to be given, it becomes necessary to resort to guess-work, rumors and supposition to fill in the voids, and none of them will ever be rectified, they will stay on the reader's memory. How many hasty, immature, superficial and misleading judgments are expressed every day, confusing readers, without any verification. The press can both stimulate public opinion and miss-educate it. Thus we may see terrorists heroized, or secret matters, pertaining to one's national defense, publicly revealed, or may witness shameless intrusion on the privacy of well-known people under the slogan, "everyone is entitled to know everything". But this is a false slogan, characteristic of a false era: people also have the right not to know, and it is a much more valuable one. The right not to have their divine souls stuffed with gossip, nonsense, vain talk. A person who works and leads a meaningful life does not need this excessive burdening flow of information.

Solzhenitsyn concludes by saying:

Hastiness and superficiality are the psychic-disease of the 20th century and more than anywhere else this disease is reflected in the process. In-depth analysis of a problem is anathema to the press. It stops at sensational formulas.

Such as it is, however, the press has become the greatest power within the Western countries, more powerful than the legislature, the executive and the judiciary. One would then like to ask: by what law has it been elected and to whom is it responsible? In the communist east a journalist is frankly appointed as a state official. But who has granted Western journalists their power, for how long a time and with what prerogatives? (1)

In 1981 - only two short years after Solzhenitsyn spoke at Harvard University - two social scientists, Robert Lichter and Stanley Rothman, released a blockbuster survey of 240 journalists of America's most prestigious and influential media outlets (ABC, NBC, CBS, PBS, The New York Times, The Washington Post, Time, Newsweek, etc) about their political views and voting patterns. (2)

The published survey in a 1981 issue of *Public Opinion* clearly demonstrated that the American media (broadcasters and journalists) held overwhelmingly liberal positions on a wide range of political and social issues. The survey of "Media and Business Elites" received wide spread coverage in the 80's and is still regarded today as one of the most accurate and insightful views of the American media. Because of its rare and candid look at the media, not many other similar in-depth surveys have been conducted. This is most likely because it gives a crystal clear picture of just where the power brokers of the American media really stand.

Following is a brief comparison in the Lichter-Rothman Survey of how the average American citizen compares to the top 240 media (writers, producers, reporters and executives) on a brief list of social issues.

Adultery
- Only 15% of the media elites strongly agreed & 32% agreed with a statement that adultery is wrong
- 85% of American said adultery is morally wrong.

Abortion
- 90% of the media elites agreed or strongly agreed that a woman has a right to abortion.
- 65% of average Americans believe that abortion is morally wrong.

Homosexuality
- Only 24% of media elites agreed or strongly agreed that homosexuality is wrong.
- 71% of Americans feel homosexuality is morally wrong. (3)

The previously mentioned Harris Poll conducted in December 2008 on the abortion issue reflects that the

American people continue to want all or most abortions to be illegal and that overwhelming majority of Americans want more protection limits in the law for the unborn child. On the issue of homosexuality or same sex marriage, 31 out 31 states have spoken by their votes and said marriage is between one man and one woman. The media elites even back in 1981 who created the news and beamed it into your living rooms every evening were totally out of touch with the American people. Most every independent media watch dog group reports they are even more out of touch with the average American citizen today. Don't hold your breath for another full-scale candid survey of media elites such as the Lichter-Rothman survey in 1981 any time soon because it will blow their cover. The American public would see just how out of touch they are with main stream America.

Another articulate voice weighing in on the impact of the media on Christian life in America is Archbishop Charles J. Chaput. He recently addressed the American Bible Society in New York in May, 2009 and said,:

> The American news and entertainment media, which now so often overlap, are the largest catechetical syndicate in history. Saying the media has helped create a culture based on "immediacy, brevity, visual stimulation, celebrity and self absorption," he warned this has great implications for the Christian's place in American society...."The lesson of St. Paul, now and for every generation, is that we need to

engage the world with intelligence, a creative spirit and most importantly, charity, which "bears all things, believes all things, hopes all things, endures all things." Real charity depends on truth, not "shallow courtesies" and "false compromises. (4)

Back in 1980, President Reagan swept into office with a landslide victory and the pro-life movement was energized with a truly pro-life President. He later wrote in his 1984 book *Abortion and the Conscience of the Nation* that "abortion concerns not only the unborn child, it concerns every one of us." (5) At that point I decided to head off to Washington D.C. and find out for myself just how our U.S. Congressman and Senators felt about the abortion issue. I remember specifically one encounter with Senator Adlai Stevenson, Jr., one of my U.S. Senators from Illinois. I asked Senator Stevenson what his position was on abortion and specifically the 1973 Roe versus Wade Supreme Court decision. I was rather dumbfounded when he said "he was still studying the case and he hadn't really come to a final decision." (6) I remember saying something to the effect of "how many years do you need to come to some kind of decision?"

I arrived in Washington D.C. on January 21st the day before the "March for Life" and as I looked down Constitution Avenue on January 22nd (the anniversary date of Roe versus Wade), I witnessed a sea of people which extended for miles (or as far as the eye could see). I asked a police officer who had crowd control duty that day how many people he estimated were there in the March. Without any hesitation he said "this is one of the largest crowds I have ever seen in my life here in Washington and I would guess somewhere between 750,000 to 1,000,000 people." (7) The next day I arrived back in my home state of Illinois fully expecting the local daily newspapers in the Chicago area to give front page coverage to such a huge gathering of citizens in our nation's capital. To my surprise, all the Chicago daily newspapers pretty much buried the story. In fact, one newspaper said that 3,500 pro-lifers marched in Washington D.C. I thought to myself they only missed the real count by only 750,000 people!

It is hard to believe just how biased the main stream secular media really has become and how many Americans still put their full faith and trust in the media. I believe Mark Twain, an American known for his plain talk and common sense, once said, "If you don't read the newspapers you are uninformed. If you do read the newspapers you are misinformed." Fortunately today there are other sources of obtaining the news besides newspapers but the key question is why can't we just receive the news, the facts and especially the truth without all the media bias? Americans need to realize that they are systematically being denied the truth because of how the elite, secular news organizations believe America should be run.

I believe the long-term solution is to get men and women of integrity like Henry Luce, the founder of *Time Magazine*, back in charge of running these operations. Luce was an executive and editor who insisted on the moral responsibility of his company to always operate in the public interest. It was at this point in my life that I realized the mainstream elite media was running interference for the abortion movement and I needed to be creative in getting the pro-life message out to the people. The mainstream media was clearly not doing the job.

By 1979 I knew I had to do something as millions of unborn babies had been killed since the 1973 *Roe vs Wade* decision. But what? I realized that, even though this genocide was taking place, the American public was being screened out by the media. I decided to make a pro-life documentary film with expert testimony in the fields of medicine, counseling, fetal development of the unborn child, and religion (what did the bible say about abortion and the taking of innocent human life?). Then I would get the film on T.V for millions to see.

The first thing I did was to see what T.V. stations in the Chicago area might carry such a program. I thought my best option was a local evangelical T.V. station that had an advertised market of 15 million potential viewers. I started trying to contact Jerry Rose, the president of the organization.

After about 25 phone calls I finally got through to him and set up a meeting with him in Chicago. At the meeting Jerry Rose agreed to give me 1☐ hours of prime time T.V. at no cost, but I had to produce and pay for the program myself.

I then looked around to see who could produce such a program. There was one local studio capable of producing such a program for me and that was Olympic Studios on the west side of Chicago. I set up a meeting with the president of Olympic Studios and brought along Joe Sheidler for moral support. After I explained what I wanted to produce, we got down to the financial details. He told me how many cameramen would be needed and how many hours it would take to produce. The final projected cost was $12,000.

Since my wife and I had only been married a couple of years and our son and daughter were both under three years old, we only had $5,000 in the whole world. So I said, "I can pay you $5,000 in cash."

There was a dead silence in the room. Finally he looked at me and said "if you can get all of your people in town for one day of filming, we have a deal".

The first person I called was Bill Berg, a nationwide radio talk show host on WGN RADIO. I had never met Bill, but after listening to him for several years on the radio, I knew he was pro-life.

Next I called Dr. Eugene Diamond, a leading gynecologist at Loyola University, who had written a book on the dangers of abortion to women.

I then called 2 leading Pro-life Evangelical Ministers - Dr. Harold O.J. Brown & Dr. Joel Naderhood. Father Frank Pavone of Priests for Life said, "Dr. Harold O.J. Brown was a giant in the struggle against the culture of death." (8) Dr. Joel Naderhood had his own evangelical T.V. program and he constantly spoke out against the evils of abortion.

Finally I asked Joe Scheidler to find me two women who had an abortion and who deeply regretted their decisions. They agreed to be interviewed by a professional counselor for our T.V. documentary.

In addition to all our speakers, we turned the documentary into a Pro-Life Fund Raiser by setting the stage up with a backdrop of telephone callers such as you see in a telethon.

We then took out a full page ad in the Chicago Tribune with pictures of all our speakers so we could attract as many viewers as possible.

Finally we completed shooting and editing the 1☐ hour pro-life T.V. documentary.

A few of the results of pro-life documentary:

1) We raised just over $5,000 from the T.V. Telethon–almost the exact amount I put in. None of the nationally known pro-life leaders charged us one penny for their time and services.

2) Joe Scheidler called me several days after the documentary aired and told me that 15 women had called into his office and they decided not to go through with their abortions after watching the program.

3) Jerry Rose liked the program so much that he ran it again one year later on prime time TV.

CHAPTER 6.

Culture versus the Economy

James Carville served as President Clinton's campaign strategist in 1992 and left President Clinton a note one day that said, "It's the economy, stupid". Carville believed and millions of American Catholics also agreed by their vote in the November 2008 election that the most salient issue in the Presidential election was the economy. Politicians and the mainstream media tended to push this idea but unfortunately millions of Catholics also believed it, making that their major criteria for electing our 44th President of the United States.

Back in the fall of 2006, I wrote a letter that was published in a major Chicago area paper that asked the question why were so many people who knew very little about Barack Obama hailing him as the next "Messiah" and the "next coming" without knowing almost anything about him except that he was charismatic and was calling for hope and change. Normally, when we make major decisions on prospective candidates, we look at their experience, their character, their ability to lead, their ability to make tough decisions, etc. but Obama was the least experienced candidate to become a major party's nominee. At that time he had only been an Illinois State Senator for 6 years.

Just prior to the 2004 election, a Cato Institute study conducted by Ilya Somin, an assistant professor of law at George Mason University, concluded that "voters are ignorant about the candidates and their positions and do not know enough about the issues to make an informed choice on November 2nd." (1)

The question all Americans, and especially Catholics who take their voting choices seriously, is: how can we in a truly free country make informed decisions about candidates, issues and policies if we know very little or almost nothing about them except for the 30 second media sound bites that emanate from manipulative media experts? I believe this idea reinforces the fact that we as freedom loving Americans need to make better use of our God-given gifts of intellect (reason and analysis) and will (our capacity to choose and love). We need to look beyond the trivial sound bites and truly "think outside the box", going around the elite media. We must use our solid Catholic teaching and morals that have withstood the test of time (long before any of our governments or media even existed) and witness to the truth of our Catholic faith.

I believe that our culture is key to our future in America. It is the whole package: it is our beliefs, our ideas, our customs, the arts, education, our skills and our values. It is what defines us as Americans; it is everything. I believe totally focusing on our financial and economic concerns is a simplistic and shortsighted view that essentially will lead to the loss of our Christian culture and heritage.

As I reflect back on my life which has been full (at times exciting and hectic), the two events that shocked me the most was: (1) hearing that President John F. Kennedy was assassinated in 1963 (2) the collapse of Communism and the breach of the Berlin Wall in 1989. Years ago during my studies of European history, I was convinced that Communism would be with us certainly throughout my lifetime and for the foreseeable future.

John Paul II certainly played a pivotal role in the collapse of European communism. Many astute observers say it all began with his pilgrimage to Poland in 1979 when he reminded the Poles of their value as Christians. His message created a "revolution of conscience" which led to the political revolution of 1989.

This revolution, according to the pope, "was made possible by a prior moral and cultural revolution, which created the conditions for the possibility for the non-violent political upheaval that swept Marxism-Leninism into the dustbin of European history." (2)

In June 1997, John Paul II returned to his beloved Poland and, even though most observers focused on the gigantic crowds (over 1.2 million in Krakow alone on June 8th), the salient message that he beamed to his fellow Poles was the "priority of culture over politics and economics and his Vatican II driven sense of the "public church" as, essentially the shaper of cultures". (3)

The pope's analysis was designed to not only alert all seven of Western Europe's newly reunified democracies but also to all western societies:

> That politics was not just a matter of winning elections...nor was the success of economic reform to be measured solely by the indices of gross national product. Rather, the greatness of the role of political leaders is to act always with respect for the dignity of every human being, to create the conditions of a generous solidarity which never marginalizes any citizen, to permit each individual to have access to culture, to recognize and put into practice the loftiest human and spiritual values, to profess and to share one's religious beliefs. (4)

Another major theme of his pontificate was how western cultures including the United States have embraced consumerism and materialism. He said, "Christ alone can free men from what enslaves him to evil and selfishness: from the frenetic search for material possessions, from the thirst for power and control over others and over things, ... from the frenzy of consumerism and hedonism which ultimately destroy the human being." (5) As one example of what this Pope was saying regarding the destruction of the human being from consumerism and greed, we see in the United States where thousands of people were bilked out of billions of dollars and it resulted in the suicide of two people who were linked to the recent Bernie Madoff scandal. Materialism leads to the loss of human dignity.

General Lewis W. Walt, who led the United States Marines during three wars and is one of our most decorated and honored Marine Generals, seems to echo the Pope's sentiments in his book, *The Eleventh Hour*. "The culture in the United States today reflects fundamentally a materialistic set of values: money, things which money can buy, physical comfort, things which satisfy our senses. Our culture is telling us that man was born to be well fed, sensually satisfied, and pleasantly amused."

As we place most of our trust in material things and drift away from God we see a direct loss of courage in our fellow countryman. General Walt goes on to say that:

> People complain in private about the state of affairs but will not speak out in public; they are afraid. Fear and courage are both reflections of value systems. The coward values his life more than his honor and duty, more than his life and so faces danger. The brave man is no more eager to die than the coward; he simply values other things more than his life so that when faced with a choice, he chooses to risk his life rather than sacrifice his other values. The trouble with materialism is that it places the individual at the center of the universe and this is a great mistake. (6)

In a democracy, it is said you get the kind of government you deserve. In George Washington's farewell address he reminded us that "Of all the dispositions and habits which lead to political prosperity; religion and morality are indispensable supports. He called these the great pillars of human happiness, the firmest props of the duties of men and citizens." (7)

Here we have two of the greatest men in history, John Paul the Great and our first, and many believe, our greatest President, George Washington, saying basically the same thing. That our greatness as a country and as human beings is not economic but it is about our faith in God and our moral values. If we are going to carry on the great legacy that our founding fathers established recognizing that there is no such thing as the authority of government separate from the authority of God, then we must take our life as citizens of this great land seriously and not be afraid to speak out publicly about what concerns us most: life, our families, and our ultimate happiness. We are all part of a struggle for our nation's future and we must not just "talk a good game" but actively participate in the public arena as God wants us to do and as our founders of this nation certainly did. It is a well-known fact that our founders were men and women of faith who were proud of that fact and who acted on their beliefs in the public arena. The key question, I believe, that confronts approximately 67 million American citizens who call themselves Catholic is when are we going to confront the truth that all life is sacred and a gift of God?

Paul Johnson, an English historian, summarizes this issue well if one is going to give real witness as a Catholic in the world.

> "The Catholic Church has not survived and flourished over 2 millennia by being popular. It has survived because what it taught is true. The quest for popularity as opposed for the quest for truth is bound to fail. Roman Catholicism is not a market research religion. In the past, Roman Catholicism has never hesitated to court unpopularity. It is not in the business to count heads or take votes. In its sacred economy quantitative principals do not apply.

Dogma and morals are not susceptible to guidance by opinion polls. The truth is paramount and it must be the naked truth." (8)

John Paul II concluded his pastoral visit to America in 1987 by saying, "Ultimately, God will not judge our nation on its economic prosperity, military strength, or international influence and prestige, but on how well it promotes and protects the dignity of every human being. May the Judge of Nations not find us wanting." (9)

In the end it boils down for all of us to the same question Thomas More faced in his English prison. Am I going to stand up for the truth (Jesus said, "I am the Truth") or am I going to be misled by the superficial media and the notion that the economy is all that really matters? Thomas More, being a man of solid faith who had an informed conscience, chose to witness to the truth and became a martyr and a saint. That is the real message that transcends this book - we need to become saints. A saint is someone who puts God first in his life not just when it is convenient or politically correct; but always. A saint is like anyone one of us, who fails and gets back up, again and again, but he never gives up always trying to put Christ ahead of his own personal wants and desires. One of my favorite authors, Frances Fernandez, eloquently makes this point, "Heaven is full of great sinners who decided to repent. Jesus always welcomes us and rejoices to see us set out again upon the road we had abandoned, perhaps in small matters." (10)

Real love is impossible without sacrifice, a love that comes from knowing Christ and looking at the Cross. The deepest meaning of our life is that we know and love Jesus and that we proclaim it to others. John Paul II explained that real love involves "a total gift of oneself" to both Christ and to others. A saint finds strength in what Christ said: "Be not afraid".

CHAPTER 7.

Whom Has America Forgotten?

Thomas More had refused to accept the claim that King Henry VIII was the head of the Church of England, thus denying the Pope's authority. When he was about to be executed after being imprisoned in the Tower of London for one year he said, "I die the King's good servant but God's first." (1)

Thomas More, by this singular act of courage, declared to the world that if God is not our first love and our first priority then life is truly not worth living. More's accomplishments are legendary:
- London's most sought after lawyer
- a loving husband and father

- Speaker of the House of Commons and the first proponent of political free speech
- Lord Chancellor, the highest appointed office
- a respected judge; eventually Chief Justice-a much imitated educator, a champion of women's education
- a well loved citizen; "born for friendship", "the best friend the poor ever had"
- an accomplished diplomat, orator, and politician opposed to absolute monarchy
- a poet and writer, famous throughout Europe, and author of the literary classic, *Utopia*. (2)

More, being a man of solid faith with the aid of an informed conscience, knew that all the gold, jewels, titles and honors that the world could bestow were not worth anything if God was not at the center and core of our lives.

The church proclaimed Thomas More a Saint in 1935 and Pope John Paul II named him to be the Patron of Statesmen and Politicians in 2000. More's life is a testament to the ages that there must be a "priority of order" in our lives if they are to have any real meaning. The words of the Gospel could not be any clearer or to the point than when Mark says "for what does it profit a man, if he gains the whole world, but suffers the loss of his own soul". (Mark 8: 36)

Just as More realized that we must put God first in our lives ahead of the acquisition of material wealth and power, Alexander Solzhenitsyn echoed this sentiment in his commencement address at Harvard University in 1978. He concludes that the primary decline of the West, is in the fact that America has forgotten God. He comments that "everything beyond physical well being and accumulation of material goods, all other human requirements and characteristics of a subtler and higher nature, were left outside the area of attention of state and social systems as if human life did not have any superior sense."

Solzhenitsyn zeroes in on the spiritual and moral decline of the west as few have done before or since when he says:

> the west kept advancing steadily in accordance with its proclaimed social intentions, hand in hand with a dazzling progress in technology. And all of a sudden it found itself in its present state of weakness. This means that the mistake must be at the root, at the very foundation of thought in modern times. I refer to the prevailing western view of the world in modern times.... It becomes the basis for political and social doctrine and could be called rationalistic humanism....the pro-claimed and practiced autonomy of man from any higher force above him. It could also be called anthropocentricity, with man seen as the center of all. (3)

Benedict XVI likewise addresses the issue of placing God first in our lives when he says in his recent book *Jesus of Nazareth*:

> when God is regarded as a secondary matter that can be set aside temporarily or permanently on account of more important things, it is precisely these supposedly more important things that come to nothing…..the issue is the primacy of God. The issue is acknowledging that He is a reality, that He is the Reality without which nothing else can be good. History cannot be detached from God and then run smoothly on purely material lines. If man's heart is not good, then nothing else can turn out good, either. And the goodness of the human heart can ultimately come only from the One who is Goodness, who is the Good itself. (4)

America has been the envy of the world with its rich natural beauty, abundant resources, unlimited food supply, and fantastic wealth but now America in its last 50 years has become a spiritually weak and morally corrupt nation. Unfortunately many judge America strictly on exterior appearances such as wealth, power and military strength. The real strength of a nation lies in its people. Are they courageous, generous, hard working, able to sacrifice, and merciful for others? Are they a people of faith?

The most astute observer of early America, Alexis de Tocqueville, in *Democracy in America* (1835), observed "I do not know whether all Americans have a sincere faith in their religion, for who can read the human heart? But I am certain that they do hold it to be indespensible to the maintenance of republican institutions. This opinion is not peculiar to a class of citizens or to a party, but it belongs to the whole Nation and to every rank of society." (5)

We do know from our history as it is well documented that our founders were men and women of faith who established this great republic with great sacrifice, many giving their very lives so that we might live. At some point millions of Americans have by their lack of faith or secular distractions have decided that they don't need God anymore. I believe most people are not consciously rejecting God but the end result is that God has been pushed to the sidelines. This is a time in our history when He is needed perhaps more than ever as our path to our ultimate salvation.

Former Supreme Court nominee Judge Robert Bork commented on the moral and spiritual condition of the United States in 2009. He said that America is "now going down a path towards kind of a happy-go-lucky nihilism… A lot of people are nihilists, "They don't think about religion. They don't think about ultimate questions. They go along. They worry about consumer goods, comfort and so forth." (6)

A recent wide-ranging study on American religious life supports the notion that when people no longer believe in God they abandon their religious practice. It found that the percentage of Christians in the nation has declined and more people say they have no religion at all. Fifteen percent of respondents said they had no religion, up from 14.2 percent in 2001 and 8.2 percent in 1990. (7)

There is an old axiom in geometry that the whole is equal to the sum of all its parts. This can be reflected by approximately 50 million abortions since 1973, divorce skyrocketing to 50% of married couples, 40% of births coming outside of marriage, and gay marriage spreading throughout the country (as of April 2009, four states, including Iowa, are allowing same sex couples to wed).

These nation-wide statistics unfortunately include Catholics who by percentage are in perfect step with these anti-life, and anti-marriage trends. Catholics are having abortions, divorcing, having children outside marriage and supporting gay marriage at the relative same rates as the rest of the population.

From a political point of view America has just elected in 2008 the most anti-life president in its history. President Obama's anti-life record was crystal clear to anyone who had ears to hear as he confirmed it on numerous campaign appearances including a nation-wide television debate seen by millions.

Following is just a few examples of his anti-life comments and votes as an Illinois State Senator, U.S. Senator from Illinois and as President (as of April 2009):

- Infanticide - supported abortion on demand through all nine months of pregnancy. He also failed to support a ban on the gruesome practice of live birth abortion (SB 1661, 1662, 1663) and partial birth abortions (HB: 382). (8)
- Traditional marriage - Senator Obama said "I will oppose any proposal to amend the Constitution to ban gays and lesbians from marrying." (Windy City Times, 4/2/04)
- Pornography - Senator Obama voted against making school boards equip computers with filtering software to prevent minors from gaining access to explicit materials. (Illinois HB 1812).
- "Freedom of Choice Act" (FOCA) – this act seeks to make abortion a fundamental right thus preventing any common sense restrictions and regulations. This is the most radical and divisive pro-abortion bill ever introduced in Congress. FOCA would overturn many existing policies including laws protecting parental

involvement and conscience rights. It would also prohibit the banning of partial birth abortion and would greatly increase tax payer funded abortions through Medicaid. (9)

The other disconnect that is occurring is not only limited to Catholics voting for candidates with views clearly contrary to Church teaching but it is the fact that millions are supporting anti-Catholic public policies at the ballot box with their votes. As an example, California's Proposition 71 was approved by voters, including millions of Catholics, to put $3 billion toward therapeutic cloning research and experiments with embryonic stem cells. This was a victory for science over religion. This is a bogus notion that science is our savior and answers all our questions and concerns. Dinesh D'Souza, in his book *What's So Great About Christianity,* questions our reliance on science: "It is time to point out a serious problem with our understanding of modern science. The problem is not with modern science itself but with a failed view of science; the idea that science is a complete framework for understanding man and the universe so that unscientific claims and ideas should be automatically rejected." (10)

The Catechism of the Catholic Church more fully elaborates on this point.

> Science and technology are precious resources when placed at the service of man and promoting his integral development for the benefit of all. By themselves however they cannot disclose the meaning of existence and of human progress. Science and technology are ordered to man, from whom they take their origin and development; hence they find in the person and in his moral values both evidence of their purpose and awareness of their limits... They must be at the service of the human person, of his inalienable rights, of his true and integral good, in confirmation with the plan and will of God. (11)

In just another example of how America (in this case the federal government with the tacit approval of an apathetic public) has sold out to the false notion that "science is our savior", we hear that the Federal Drug Association (FDA) will now allow seventeen-year olds to buy the "morning after" emergency contraceptive without a doctor's prescription. U.S. District Judge Edward Korman ordered the FDA to let 17 year-olds get these birth control pills. He also directed the agency to evaluate whether all age restrictions should be lifted. "It's a good indication that the agency will move expeditiously to ensure its policy of Plan B is based solely on science," said Nancy Northrup, President of the Center for Reproductive Rights, which filed the lawsuit. (12)

We cannot and must not separate scientific research and progress from its intrinsic moral and ethical foundation or it becomes nothing but phony science which is misleading at best and destructive to the common good for our whole society. If we divorce scientific advances from its ethical foundation we have not advanced as so many in our society believe but we have taken another step towards the ultimate break down of our culture of life.

Even though many seek to elevate science above faith, subjugating or even replacing it altogether, President Obama has sought to twist and leverage the notion of faith in order to promote recent public policies. A perfect example is where he has decided to lift the ban on the use of embryonic stem cell research using his faith as a partial justification. Cal Thomas, nationally syndicated journalist, responds by saying:

> in classical style of a brilliant politician, President Obama sought to invoke an ethical standard for his decision, while simultaneously denying a standard that might restrain scientists from going too far. He said that as a "person of faith", he believes we are called to care for each other and work to ease human suffering. I believe we have been given the capacity and will to pursue this research—and the humanity and conscience to do so responsibly... President Obama wants a "faith" unconnected to anything outside of himself to advance his policy on stem cell research.

These policies come to us despite the fact that adult stems cells have proven highly successful with thousands of cures and the University of California at Los Angeles has confirmed that human skin cells (which engender no moral debate) can be converted to stem cells which are virtually identical to the embryonic variety. Thomas continues:

> we have been warned by history in novels like Aldous Huxley's "brave new world" "...of what can happen when government operates outside a moral code established to protect us from its penchant to be excessive. Unfortunately, government in recent years has sometimes engaged in a type of freelancing, embracing a mushy morality in order to serve purposes that are sometimes immoral. (13)

The thought that science reigns supreme forgets the key ingredient that God is our Creator and our Savior. The first commandment that God gave to us through Moses was to love God first and not to be fooled by false idols (and theories) that contradict God's law.

The Catechism of The Catholic Church again helps to clarify this issue that has confused many.

> "What moves us to believe is not the fact that revealed truths appear as true and intelligible in the light of our natural reason: we believe "because of the authority of God himself who reveals them, who can neither deceive nor be deceived...Faith is certain. It is more certain than all human knowledge because it is founded on the very word of God who cannot lie. Ten thousand difficulties do not make one doubt." (14)

Then we need to ask ourselves are we truly living and proclaiming our Catholic faith in America? We need to take another look at how we are living our Catholic lives and ask do we truly believe the major tenets of our Catholic faith? We study for school (elementary, high school and college), for our jobs and for military service, but when is the last time we studied the New Testament, the Old Testament, the Catechism of the Catholic Church or any of the Church's great encyclicals? We cannot teach what we don't know ourselves.

The first step is to live a life of personal sanctity or union with God. This one act of the will is the greatest step you can take in your life today: to seek Christ, to find Christ, to fall in love with Christ and to stay with Christ.

We see this huge disconnect between people who call themselves Catholic and the lives they live. Their Catholicism is not reflected in the candidates whom they choose to elect or the public policies that they support. Are we really a nation of faith as all the statistics tell us? Or are millions of Catholics merely wearing a mask? These questions take us full circle in this book as we asked the question in the first chapter, What did the recent elections teach us and how can people who call themselves Catholic vote for the most pro-abortion candidate ever to run for the Presidency of the United States? We have a real dichotomy in this country between what a Catholic is supposed to believe and profess and what actually is manifested in our American culture today.

There are approximately 30 million lapsed Catholics in America today. If this group were its own religious denomination, it would be the second largest religious group in the whole country. We do not have a robust, healthy Catholic culture in America today. Catholics need to live out in today's world the fullness of their faith. When this happens, we will have a culture where our political officials and public policies will respect the sanctity of human life.

John Paul II in 1987 finished his pastoral visit to the United States by challenging us to be the people that God created us to be, to live our Christian life to the full and to "be not afraid". He said, "For this reason, America your deepest identity and truest character as a nation is revealed in the position you take toward the human person. The ultimate test of your greatness is the way you treat every human being, but most especially the weakest and most defenseless ones." (15)

If we truly believe the departing words of our Lord when he said "I am with you all days (always), even to the consummation of the world". What else do we need to know except that Jesus is telling us in his own words that "you are a chosen race, a royal priesthood, a holy nation, a purchased people; that you may proclaim the perfection of Him who has called you out of darkness into his marvelous light." 1 Peter 2-9,10.

CHAPTER 8.

Changing Our Existing Culture of Death to a Culture of Life

Will our nation finally turn back to God? Will our country once again truly be "One Nation Under God" ? Only God knows the answer to that question but we do know that as Catholics, we can make a difference and change our existing culture of death which has now taken 50 million unborn babies since 1973 to a culture of life if we truly put God first in our lives and become fully engaged in our culture.

C.S. Lewis explains the essence of Christianity when he says "I believe in Christianity as I believe that the sun has risen: not only because I see it, but because by it I see everything else." (1) It illuminates our whole life.

The first step is always to use prayer and the sacraments to ask for God's intercession in this great issue of defending the life of the innocent, our unborn brothers and sisters.

Here are a few suggestions:

1) Prayer—It is the most powerful weapon we have. When Christ walked the face of this earth He constantly stressed the need for prayer, a personal conversation with God. Prayer is raising our hearts and minds to God. It is indispensable in everything we do. The real joy of life is to be near our Lord. Author Frances Fernandez comments on prayer:

> St. Paul gives us the key to understanding the origin of any unhappiness we may feel: it comes from putting a distance between ourselves and God, through our sins, through tepidity. Our Lord always brings joy and affliction. His mysteries are all joyful mysteries, the sorrowful mysteries we bring on ourselves." Hail, full of grace, the Lord is with you," (Luke 1:28) said the Angel to Mary. It is the nearness of God which makes the virgin rejoice. And the nearness of the Messiah will make the unborn Baptist show forth his joy in the womb of Elizabeth. (Luke 2:4) And the angel will say to the shepherds: "Be not afraid; for behold, I

bring you good news of a great joy which will come to all the people; for to you is born this day a Savior" (Luke 2:10-11)... Joy is to possess Jesus; unhappiness is to lose him. (2)

The *Navarre Bible Series* and *In Conversation with God* by Frances Fernandez are two excellent selections if your objective is to get closer to Christ.

2) Receive the Sacraments—They are a fountain of grace. Especially the Holy Eucharist which is a share in the divine life (Christ's life in us). John Paul II said in the Apostolic Exhortation, *Ecclesia in America*: "The Eucharist is the living and lasting center around which the entire community of the Church gathers". (3) We are saved by God's grace and we cannot get to heaven without God's grace. The holy sacrifice of the mass is the highest form of worship. It is the renewal on our alters of Our Lord's sacrifice on calvary of his body and blood. Just one mass gives God more praise and thanksgiving than the combined worship of all the angels and saints.

Just one mass has greater power of atoning for sin than all the sacrifices of all the faithful on earth. Just one mass can do more for the souls in purgatory than all our prayers for them and all their own sufferings.

Hearing mass daily can help you:

-To avoid temptation and sin

-To find peace amid the trials of life

-To grow in the love of God

-To thank God for all his blessings

-To obtain protection against all dangers

-To gain the favors of which you stand in need

-To shorten the purgatory of your dear departed ones

-To find out what God wants for you

The greatest daily event in your neighborhood is the Holy Sacrifice of the Mass you attend.

3) Spiritual Reading—We all need to be nourished by good books. The New Testament cannot be beaten if our objective is to identify ourselves with the words and actions of Christ. A few titles you may consider: "This Tremendous Lover" by Eugene Boylan, "Christ is Passing By" by Josemaria Escriva de Balaguer, "Mere Christianity" by C.S. Lewis.

4) Educate yourself in your Catholic Faith. All the tenets of our Catholic Faith are available in the *Catechism of*

the Catholic Church. It is a veritable fountain of truth and knowledge. *Faith and Reason* by JP II explains the relationship between faith and reason. Benedict XVI in his University of Regensburg address clearly affirms that faith without reason is totally unacceptable and that the Catholic Church has always taught and still does that faith insists on being founded on reason.

5) Catholic Moral Teaching—John Paul II's *The Splendor of Truth* answers the most fundamental moral questions that Catholics and all men and women who seek the truth are committed to finding. "THE TRUTH SHALL SET YOU FREE".

6) Human Life— *The Gospel of Life* by JP II focuses on the sacredness, value and inviolability of human life. Congressman Henry Hyde said:
> When the time comes as it surely will, when we face that awesome moment, the final judgment, I've often thought, as Fulton Sheen wrote, that it is a terrible moment of loneliness. You have no advocates, you are there alone standing before God—and a terror will rip your soul like nothing you can imagine. But I really think that those in the pro-life movement will not be alone. I think there'll be a chorus of voices that have never been heard in this world but are heard beautifully and clearly in the next world—and they will plead for everyone who has been in this movement.

They will say to God, 'Spare him, because he loved us,' – and God will look at you and say not, "Did you succeed?' but 'Did you try?" (4)

7) How could we end our plan to change our culture of death to a culture of life without appealing to Mary, our Mother and the Mother of God.

The first Catholic Archbishop of the United States, John Carroll, in 1792 dedicated and permanently entrusted this new Republic and all it's citizens to Jesus Christ through Mary, His Mother.

Consecration of the United States of America to Mary

"Most Holy Trinity, Our Father in Heaven, Who chose Mary as the fairest of your daughters; Holy Spirit Who chose Mary as your Spouse; God the Son Who choose Mary as your Mother, In union with Mary, we adore Your Majesty and acknowledge your supreme, eternal dominion and authority. Most Holy Trinity, we place the United States of America into the hands of Mary Immaculate in order that she may present the country to You. Through her we wish to thank You for the great resources of this land and for the freedom which has been its heritage.

Through the intercession of Mary, have mercy on the Catholic Church in America. Grant us peace. Have mercy on our President and on all the officers of our government.

Grant us a fruitful economy, born of justice and labor. Protect the family life of the nation. Guard the precious gift of many religious vocations. Through the intercession of Mary our Mother, have mercy on the sick. The tempted, sinners….on all who are in need.

Mary, Immaculate Virgin, Our Mother. Patroness of our land, we praise and honor you and give ourselves to you. Protect us from every harm. Pray for us, that acting always according to your will and the will of your Divine Son, we may live and die pleasing to God. Amen." (5)

Action Steps

C.S. Lewis' point that faith illuminates our life makes us realize that we need to put God first in our lives. We understand however that faith alone is not enough but that it must be followed up with action to change our existing culture of death to a real culture of life. For what good is our faith if it doesn't affect how we live our lives.

Here are a few suggestions:

1. Don't underestimate the power of a personal visit, letter, or telephone call to your elected representatives. As I mentioned earlier hundreds or perhaps thousands of babies were saved in Illinois because a single state senator received many phone calls. The representatives themselves tell us that a personal visit, letter or phone call is worth many mass produced mailings.

As just one example of what can happen when the people become fully informed, as Jefferson said, they will respond.
In March 2009 Illinois HB 2354, the Reproductive Health and Access Act, steam rolled through the Illinois Human Services Committee on a 5 to 2 vote and was headed for passage in the Illinois House of Representatives. Suddenly the people became aware of this anti-life and anti-family bill and they started contacting their representatives by the thousands. In fact one state representative in the northwest suburbs of Chicago, whose office had been telling callers protesting this bill that she was planning on voting for the bill, received over 2,500 signed petitions asking her to vote against this bill. The

pressure became so intense on some legislators that the sponsors of the bill considered adding some meaningless amendments to pick up some wavering votes in the Illinois House but the people would not be denied. Finally the sponsors of the bill pulled the bill from any further consideration in the current legislative session when it became apparent that the bill had no chance of passage. This is just one small example of what the people can and must do if we are going to restore this great Republic to a culture that truly respects the dignity of all human persons (born and unborn). This temporary defeat of HB 2354 was a textbook example of the Catholic Church (Cardinal Francis George and the Catholic Conference) working together with various lay groups through out the state to defeat this bill. It is absolutely amazing what can be done when we utilize the latest Internet technology: social networking websites (such as Facebook, Twitter and LinkedIn), blogs, online petition forms, text messaging, e-mail blasts, smart phones, etc. We must become truly organized (lay and Church) working together to truly restore this nation to a culture of life. Believe me our elected representatives will hear us and they will respond. We must stay vigilant however as this is just one victory in a long war.

I believe Pope St. Leo the Great sums up this matter when he says "Christians be aware of your dignity; it is God's own nature that you share". (6)

2. If your state is not one of the 31 states that has passed a constitutional amendment - keeping marriage between one man and one woman- contact your local Catholic Archdiocese Office for more information and get involved. A key point to remember is that issues like abortion & gay marriage should transcend party and partisan politics. Just as slavery in earlier centuries fiercely divided our nation, eventually the "common good" of all its citizens was fully recognized and protected by our constitution and the rule of law. Today in America we see our country divided again on the issue of "same sex marriage".

One of the clearest examples that the people do not favor same sex marriage is the fact that in the 2008 Elections California's Proposition 8 (which would have approved gay marriage) was defeated in one of our most liberal states. The reason for the defeat was largely due to the African-American vote. Despite 96% of the African American voters choosing Barack Obama, they overwhelmingly voted against gay marriage to the tune of 70% of their votes. Americans by their faith, family and the natural moral law understand that marriage is between one man and one woman.

3. Join your local pro-life group or your local parish pro-life organization. If none exist, start your own pro-life group. Priests for Life at: www.priestsforlife.org is another resource.

4. Support a local or national pro-life counseling center such as the Women's Center in Chicago at 773-794-1313 or Birthright of Chicago at 773-233-0305.

5. Financially support pro-life groups like the National Right to Life Committee that was founded in 1973 and currently has over 3,000 chapters in the United States. As described on their website, the National Right to Life Committee has been instrumental in achieving a number of legislative reforms at the national level, including a ban on non-therapeutic experimentation of unborn and newborn babies, a federal conscience clause guaranteeing medical personnel the right to refuse to participate in abortion procedures, and various amendments to appropriations bills which prohibit (or limit) the use of federal funds to subsidize or promote abortions in the United States and overseas. The ultimate goal of the National Right to Life Committee is to restore legal

protection to innocent human life. The NRLC can be contacted in Washington D.C. at: www.nrlc.org

6. Another very effective group is The Thomas More Law Center which is a national non-profit public interest law firm whose mission is to defend in the courts of our land the religious freedom of Christians, traditional family values and the sanctity of human life. Thomas More Law Center does not charge for their services and relies on public donations. The TMLC can be contacted at 734-827-2001 or go online to: www.thomasmore.org

7. Follow the lead of John Paul II by helping to evangelize the world by passing on your faith to your family, neighbors and friends. Remember the words of John Paul the Great; "it is not enough to know Christ; you must introduce Him to others". (7)

A few common sense bits of wisdom:

Cut down on watching television. It is addictive. Read and study good books. Spend more time with your family and friends. Realize that "only dead fish go with the flow". (8)

Finally imagine that you are one of the early apostles, like St. Paul, and realize that you must stand against the tide of popular public opinion and witness to the truth.

NOTES

1. WHAT DID THE 2008 ELECTIONS TEACH US?

1. Haven Bradford Gow, "Natural Law", *Daily Herald Newspaper*, Arlington Heights, IL. (Contributing Editor of the Catholic League for Religious & Civil Rights.
2. Charles Rice, *50 Questions on the Natural Law: What it is and Why We Need It*. (San Francisco: Ignatius Press, 1993), p. 30,31.
3. John Paul II, "The Human Person—God's Greatest Blessing" in *John Paul II in America* (Boston: Daughters of St. Paul) 1987.
4. Wikipedia, (the free encyclopedia) "Roman Catholicism in the United States". November 26, 2008, p.1.
5. Ibid, Page 1.
6. Phil Lawler, "What's Wrong with Catholic Voters? What's Wrong with Catholics?", November 5, 2008, p.1.
7. Cardinal Francis George, U.S. Bishops Meeting, June, 2003, St. Louis, Missouri, p1.
8. Theodore Roosevelt, "Citizenship in a Republic", Speech at the Sorbonne, Paris, April 23, 1910.

9. Archbishop Charles J. Chaput, O.F.M., "Building and Promoting a Culture of Life", February 8, 2009, Ireland, p. 4-5

2. GETTING INVOLVED IN THE POLITICAL PROCESS

3. WHAT IS A TRULY CATHOLIC CONSCIENCE?

1. Cardinal George Pell, "The Inconvenient Conscience, *First Things Magazine*, June/July, 2006. p.1.
2. Bishop Robert Morlino, (Bishop of Madison Wisconsin), "Bishop Morlino Encourages the Faithful to Vote Pro-Life", *Crossed the Tiber*, November 05, 2006.
3. Richard John Neuhaus, "The Splendor of Truth", (Richard John Neuhaus is Editor in chief of First Things), *The Wall Street Journal*, October 8, 1993.
4. *Cathechism of the Catholic Church*, United States Catholic Conference Inc—Libreria Editrice Vaticana — English Translation for the United States of America, 1994. p.400.
5. Josemaria Escriva De Balaguer, "Marriage: A Christian Vocation", *Reprinted from Christ is Passing By*, (Chicago, Scepter Press, 1974) p. 5-6.

6. The Heritage Foundation, "Statement by Five Dutch Social Science Professors on the Deterioration of Marriage in the Netherlands", From Reformatorisch Dagblad, July 8, 2004.
7. Thomas Jefferson to Richard Price, 1789, ME 7:253
8. Dr. Amin Abboud, "Ethical Reflections on Current Affairs", Resource Center api7.com, March 4, 2005, p.1,5.
9. John Edwards, Campaign Stop in Newton, Iowa, October, 2004.
10. Archbishop Charles J. Chaput, (Archbishop's Column), Denver Catholic Register, "Embryonic Stem Cell Research and Human Dignity", Week of October 20, 2004.
11. Wesley J. Smith, "Culture of Death", (The assault on medical ethics in America). Copyright in 2000 by Wesley Smith, (San Francisco: Encounter Books) p. 9.
12. Charles Krauthammer, "Stem Cell Vindication", *The Washington Post*, November 30, 2007; A23
13. Liz Townsend, "Deceptive Cloning Initiative on November Ballot in Missouri", August 28, 2006, *St. Louis Review*.
14. Archbishop Raymond L. Burke, "Rally Against Stem Cell Initiative in Missouri", August 28, 2006, *St. Louis Review*.

15. John Haas, "The Scourge of In Vitro Fertilization", The National Catholic Bioethics Center, September 2007, p. 1, 2.
16. John Noonan, *A Private Choice*, (New York: The Free Press, A division of Macmillan Publishing Co., Inc, 1979) p.1.
17. Ronald Reagan, *Abortion and the Conscience of the Nation*, Thomas Nelson Publishers, Copyright 1984, p.8.
18. Mother Theresa, "Mother Theresa's Letter to the US Supreme Court on Roe v. Wade". This amicus brief was filled before the US Supreme Court in the cases of Loce v. New Jersey and Krail et al. v. New Jersey in February 1994 by Mother Theresa

4. JUDICIAL ACTIVISM

1. Alexander Hamilton, *Federalist Papers* 78, 81, 82,
2. Newt Gingrich, *Winning the Future*, "Bringing the Courts Back Under the Constitution" (Washington, D.C: Regnery Publishing, Inc., 2005) p.58.
3. Ibid, p. 57.
4. Life News.Com, Harris Poll of December 10-12, 2008, "Plurality of Americans Want All or Most Abortions Illegal, Want Pro-Life Laws", December 30, 2008.

5. Doug Kmiec, Professor of Pepperdine University, *Family News in Focus*, "Stick to U.S. Law, Judges told", March, 2005, p. 1.
6. Justice Anthony Kennedy, "Roper v. Simmons". Justice Kennedy's opinion on this juvenile death case, March 2005.
7. Justice Antonin Scalia, Associated Press, Hope Yen, "Scalia Slams Juvenile Death Penalty", March 15, 2005.
8. Justice Robert Bork, *Wall Street Journal*, July 5, 2005
9. Archbishop Charles J. Chaput, "Archbishop Charles J. Chaput's Canterbury Award", (Hewarns of the loss of religious freedom), May 7, 2009, New York City, N.Y., (Catholic News Agency) CNA.
10. Father Raymond J. de Souza, "Catholic Priest's Unexpected Life", *National Catholic Register*, (reported by Tom McFeely), January 9, 2009.
11. Timothy George, "The Radical Conservative", (Richard John Neuhaus helped inspire a generation of evangelicals to participate boldly in the public square), *Christianity Today*, March 11, 2009.
12. Cornell University Law School, L11/Legal Information Institute, Historic Supreme Court Decisions—by topic.
13. Henry Hyde, *For Every Idle Silence*, (Ann Arbor, Michigan: Servant Books, 1985) p. 13.

5. MEDIA

1. Alexander I. Solzhenitsy, "A World Split Apart", Commencement Address delivered at Harvard University, June 8, 1978. p. 4, 5, &7.
2. Media Research Center, "Media Bias Basics", "Journalists Political Views", (Referencing Robert Lichter and Stanley Rothman's 1981 Survey of 240 journalists at the top media outlets)
3. FrontpageMag.com, "A Statistical Analysis of Media Bias", John Perazzo, October 13, 2008. Footnotes 2 & 4. (Referencing Robert Lichter and Stanly Rothman's 1981 survey of 240 journalists at the top media outlets, Op. cit; Robert Lichter & Stanley Rothman's 1986 Study, Op.cit.
4. Archbishop Charles J. Chaput, "Arbishop Chaput: Media Culture and Compromise Undermining Christian Life", New York, New York, May 6, 2009.
5. Ronald Reagan, *Abortion and the Conscience of the Nation* (New York: Thomas Nelson Publishers, 1984), p.8. (Copyright 1984,The Human Life Foundation, Inc)
6. U.S. Senator Adali Stevenson Jr., Senate Office Building, "March for Life", Washington, D.C, January 21-22, 1980.

7. Washington D.C. Uniformed Police Officer handling crowd control for the "March for Life", on January 22, 1980.
8. Father Frank Pavone, Priests for Life, "Mourns the Death of Dr. Harold O.J. Brown, Summer, 2007.

6. CULTURE VERSUS THE ECONOMY

1. Cal Thomas, *Gwinnett Daily Post*, "When the Uninformed Make Elections a Popularity Contest, the Country Suffers", October 21, 2004. p1
2. John Paul II, Homily on Consumerism and Materialism, March 1, 1998.
3. George Weigel, "John Paul II and the Priority of Culture", Copyright of *First Things*, February 1998. p. 1.
4. Ibid, p. 2
5. Ibid, p. 8
6. General Lewis W. Walt, *The Eleventh Hour*, (New York: Caroline House Publishers, 1979), p. 30, 31.
7. George Washington's Farewell Address on September 17, 1796.
8. Paul Johnson, historian, "Quotes by Paul Johnson" from *The Quotable Paul Johnson a Topical Compilation of His Wit, Wisdom and Satire.*, P. 185.

9. John Paul II, "The Human Person — God's Greatest Blessing", In *John Paul II in America* (Boston, Daughters of St. Paul) 1987.

10. Frances Fernandez, *In Conversation with God*, (Copyright, Scepter Press, London, 2000. p. 112.

7. WHOM HAS AMERICA FORGOTTEN?

1. Saint Thomas More Society, San Diego, California, "I Die the King's Good Servant and God's First". Thomas More was executed on Tower Hill in London on July 6, 1535.
2. Gerard B. Wegemer, *Thomas More: A Portrait of Courage*, (Princeton, Scepter Publishers, 1995), Inside Front Cover.
3. Alexander I. Solzhenitsyn, "A World Split Apart", A Commentary Address at Harvard University, June 8, 1978, p. 6,7.
4. Pope Benedict XVI, *Jesus of Nazareth*, (San Francisco: Ignatius Press, 2007) p. 33.
5. Alexis de Tochqueville, *Democracy in America*, 1835.
6. Justice Robert Bork, "Cybercast News Interview", January 21, 2009, (CNA), Washington, D.C., (6).
7. "Poll: Rise in Americans with No Religion", CBS News, 3/8/2009, Source: The Program on Public Values at Trinity College in Hartford, Conn. They surveyed 54,461

English and Spanish Adults from Feb, through Nov. 2008.

8. Erick Erickson, "Barack Obama Admits He Supported Infanticide", *Human Events*, August 19, 2008.

9. Concerned Women for America, "The Obama Watch", "The first thing I'll do as President is sign the Freedom of Choice Act. That's the first thing I'd do". Barack Obama speaking to the Planned Parenthood Action Fund. July 17, 2007.

10. Dinesh D'Souza, *What's So Great About Christianity*, (Washington D.C., Regnery Publishing, Inc. 2007), p. 155.

11. *Catechism of the Catholic Church*, United States Catholic Conference Washington D.C., 1994, p. 552.

12. *Daily Herald Newspaper*, (Associated Press), "FDA Eases Restrictions for Morning After Pill", April 23, 2009, p. 9.

13. Cal Thomas, "Stem Cells and Huxley's World", *The Daily Journal*, March 24, 2009.

14 *Catechism of the Catholic Church*, United States Catholic Conference, Washington D.C., 1994, p. 42, 43.

15. John Paul II, "The Human Person-God's Greatest Blessing" in *John Paul II in America*, (Boston, Daughters of St. Paul), 1987, p.309.

8. Changing Our Existing Culture of Death to a Culture of Life

1. C.S. Lewis, "Is Theology Poetry" (The Weight of Glory), 1944. Lewis reads "Is Theology Poetry" to the Oxford University Socratic Club. It is later published in the *Socratic Digest*, Volume 3 (1945).
2. Frances Fernandez, *In Conversation with God*, (London: Scepter, 2000) p. 111-112.
3. John Paul II, *Ecclesia in America* (On the Church in the Americas), January 22, 1999. (Apostolic Exhortation).
4. Congressman Henry Hyde, "Speech to the Maryland Right to Life Convention", October 29, 1977.
5. Janice T. Connell, *Faith of Our Founding Father, The Spiritual Journey of George Washington*, (New York: Hatherleigh Press, 2004) p. 123, 124, 125.
6. "A Christian Perspective in Life", *Virtue Media*, A Christian Blog, February 22, 2009.
7. www.vocation.com, Pope St. Leo, the Great, "When he saw many of the Pharisees and Sadducees coming to his baptism".
8. Author Unknown